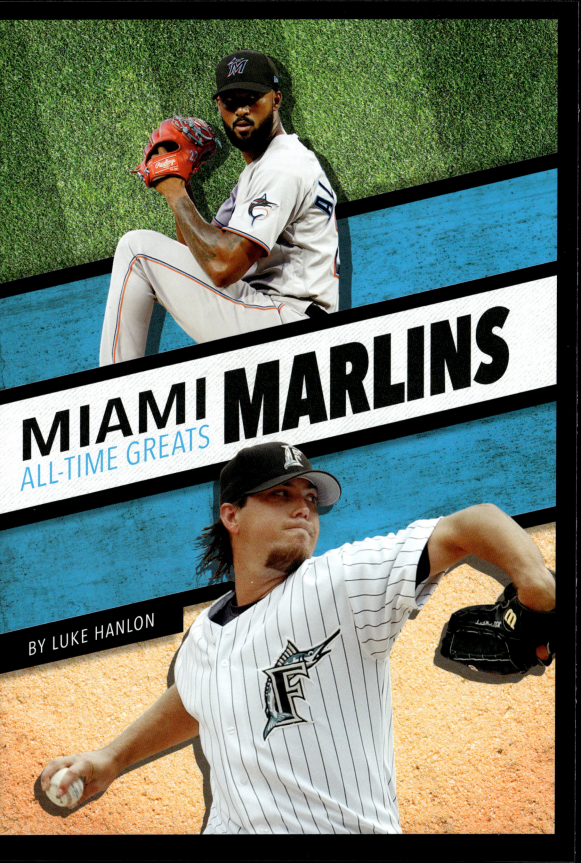

MIAMI MARLINS
ALL-TIME GREATS

BY LUKE HANLON

Copyright © 2024 by Press Room Editions. All rights reserved. No part of this book may be used or reproduced in any manner whatsoever, including internet usage, without written permission from the copyright owner, except in the case of brief quotations embodied in critical articles and reviews.

Book design by Jake Slavik
Cover design by Jake Slavik

Photographs ©: Matt Slocum/AP Images, cover (top), 1 (top); J. Pat Carter/AP Images, cover (bottom), 1 (bottom); Focus on Sport/Getty Images Sport/Getty Images, 4; Eliot J. Schechter/Allsport/Getty Images Sport/Getty Images, 7; Andy Lyons/Getty Images Sport/Getty Images, 8, 10; Jamie Squire/Getty Images Sport/Getty Images, 13; Doug Pensinger/Getty Images Sport/Getty Images, 15; Joel Auerbach/Getty Images Sport/Getty Images, 16; Mark Brown/Getty Images Sport/Getty Images, 19; Michael Reaves/Getty Images Sport/Getty Images, 21

Press Box Books, an imprint of Press Room Editions.

ISBN
978-1-63494-799-2 (library bound)
978-1-63494-819-7 (paperback)
978-1-63494-857-9 (epub)
978-1-63494-839-5 (hosted ebook)

Library of Congress Control Number: 2023910384

Distributed by North Star Editions, Inc.
2297 Waters Drive
Mendota Heights, MN 55120
www.northstareditions.com

Printed in the United States of America
012024

ABOUT THE AUTHOR

Luke Hanlon is a sportswriter and editor based in Minneapolis.

TABLE OF CONTENTS

CHAPTER 1

EXPANSION TO GLORY 5

CHAPTER 2

BACK IN OCTOBER 11

CHAPTER 3

FRESH FISH 17

TIMELINE 22

TEAM FACTS 23

MORE INFORMATION 23

GLOSSARY 24

INDEX 24

CHAPTER 1
EXPANSION TO GLORY

The Miami Marlins played their first Major League Baseball (MLB) season in 1993. Known as the Florida Marlins then, the team found a star in the expansion draft before the season. Outfielder **Jeff Conine** played every game in the team's first season. In fact, Conine became such a staple for Florida that he earned the nickname "Mr. Marlin."

The Marlins traded for another great player during the 1993 season. **Gary Sheffield** came to Florida from the San Diego Padres. Sheffield represented the Marlins at the 1993 All-Star Game. And he only got better from there. The right fielder's elite bat speed helped him become a powerful hitter. That's how he set a Marlins record with 42 home runs in 1996.

The Marlins improved in 1995 when former first-round pick **Charles Johnson** played his first full MLB season. Johnson quickly became one of the best defensive catchers in baseball, as he rarley made errors. His skills behind the plate helped Johnson win a National League (NL) Gold Glove Award in 1995. That award is given to the best defensive player at each position in the league. Johnson would win two more with the Marlins.

STAT SPOTLIGHT

WALKS IN A SEASON
MARLINS TEAM RECORD
Gary Sheffield: 142 (1996)

Kevin Brown wasn't a Marlin for long. But the starting pitcher was dominant in his short stint with Florida. In 1996, his 1.89 earned run average (ERA) was the lowest in the majors. The next season he threw a no-hitter in a 9–0 win against the San Francisco Giants.

In 1997, this core helped the Marlins make the playoffs for the first time. Starting pitcher **Liván Hernández** shined in the postseason.

In the first two rounds, he allowed only two runs in three games. Then in the World Series, he won both games he started against the Cleveland Indians.

The series went to a winner-take-all Game 7 in Florida. After falling behind 2–0, the Marlins tied the game in the bottom of the ninth inning. After a scoreless 10th inning, 21-year-old shortstop **Edgar Rentería** hit a walk-off single in the bottom of the 11th to claim the Marlins' first championship.

INSTANT SUCCESS

Jim Leyland managed the Pittsburgh Pirates for 11 seasons from 1986 to 1996. After a disappointing season in 1996, Leyland stepped down as Pittsburgh's manager. One week later, the Marlins hired him. In Leyland's first year with the team, he helped the Marlins become the fastest expansion team to win a World Series in MLB history.

CHAPTER 2
BACK IN OCTOBER

The Marlins lost most of their World Series roster in 1998. But they still had stars to build around. **Luis Castillo** made his MLB debut in 1996. The speedy second baseman broke out in 1999 with 50 stolen bases. The next season he led the NL with 62 steals. He also had an impressive .334 batting average.

STAT SPOTLIGHT

CAREER HITS
MARLINS TEAM RECORD
Luis Castillo: 1,273

Left fielder **Cliff Floyd** played his first season with the Marlins in 1997. The power hitter had his best MLB season in 2001. He hit 31 homers and posted career highs in batting average and runs batted in (RBIs). Floyd earned a trip to the All-Star Game that year.

Mike Lowell played high school and college baseball in Florida. He was drafted by the New York Yankees, but the Marlins traded for him after the 1998 season. Lowell made three All-Star teams while playing in his home state.

Lowell's best season with the Marlins was in 2003, when he hit 32 home runs and piled up 105 RBIs. The team had a few young prospects blossoming next to Lowell. **Dontrelle Willis** burst onto the scene to win the NL Rookie of the Year Award in 2003. "D-Train" used a unique delivery to fool hitters. The lefty twisted his whole body toward center field while kicking his right leg up toward his chest.

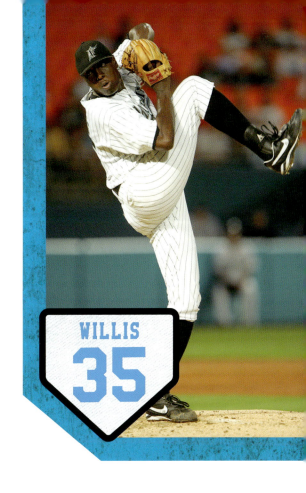

While Willis was confusing hitters, **Miguel Cabrera** was dominating opposing pitchers. The outfielder and third baseman only played about half the season in 2003. But he helped the Marlins get back to the playoffs for the first time since 1997. Cabrera led the Marlins on a great run. The rookie hit three home runs in the NL Championship Series (NLCS) against the Chicago Cubs.

That included a three-run homer in Game 7, which sent the Marlins to the World Series.

Facing the Yankees in the World Series, **Josh Beckett** was Florida's best player. The pitcher allowed just two earned runs in his two starts. With the Marlins up 3–2 in the series, Beckett took the mound at Yankee Stadium in Game 6. The righty used his fastball and curveball to strike out nine batters. Still on the mound in the ninth with two outs, a New York batter hit a

AGELESS WONDER

The Marlins started the 2003 season 16–22. The team's front office decided to make a change and hired 72-year-old Jack McKeon as the team's new manager. Fans and local media criticized the move. But five months later, McKeon became the oldest manager in MLB history to win the World Series. Dusty Baker broke McKeon's record in 2022. Baker was 73 when he led the Houston Astros to a title that year.

weak groundball in front of the mound. Beckett tagged out the runner to win the World Series for the Marlins. For his performance, Beckett won the World Series Most Valuable Player (MVP) Award.

CHAPTER 3
FRESH FISH

The Marlins struggled to find success after the 2003 World Series win. But they still had great players during that era. **Hanley Ramírez** was the best of the bunch. The talented shortstop could do a bit of everything. Ramíez had speed on the base paths and could hit consistently. Those skills earned him the NL Rookie of the Year Award in 2006.

Dan Uggla completed Florida's middle infield. The muscular second baseman loved to swing for the fences. Uggla made the All-Star Game in 2006 in his rookie season. He ended up hitting 27 home runs that year. Uggla went on to hit 30 or more homers in each of the next four seasons.

Starting pitchers **Josh Johnson** and **Aníbal Sánchez** both won 10 or more games in 2006. Sánchez made history in his 13th career start when he pitched a no-hitter against the Arizona Diamondbacks. That made him the first rookie to throw one since 2001.

Using his 6-foot-7 (201 cm) frame, Johnson overpowered hitters with his fastball. After 2006, he suffered from injuries for two seasons. But he came back strong in 2009 to make the All-Star Game. Then, in 2010, his 2.30 ERA was the best in the NL.

By 2012, the Marlins had a new look. They changed their colors from white and teal to black and orange. And they changed their name to the Miami Marlins.

Giancarlo Stanton was the leader of the new-look team. The towering right fielder looked more like a body builder than a baseball player. Stanton used his strength to belt home runs. In 2017, he led MLB with 59 of them. That earned him the NL MVP Award.

On the mound in Miami was **José Fernández**. The righty won the NL Rookie of the Year Award in 2013. He posted an ERA lower than 3.00 in every season of his career. Sadly, his life was cut short when he died in a boating accident in 2016. He was just 24 years old. By 2020, **Sandy Alcantara**

BREAKING BARRIERS

After a decade working in the Los Angeles Dodgers' front office, Kim Ng became Miami's general manager in 2020. That made Ng the first woman to be a general manager in any major professional sport in North America.

STAT SPOTLIGHT

STRIKEOUTS IN A SEASON
MARLINS TEAM RECORD
José Fernández: 253 (2016)

was Miami's newest star pitcher. That year, he helped lead the Marlins to the playoffs for the first time since 2003. "Sandman" upped his game in 2022. He led the NL with six complete games and posted an ERA of 2.28. That earned Alcantara the Cy Young Award. That is given to the best pitcher in the league each season. Miami fans hoped he could lead the team on another run to the World Series.

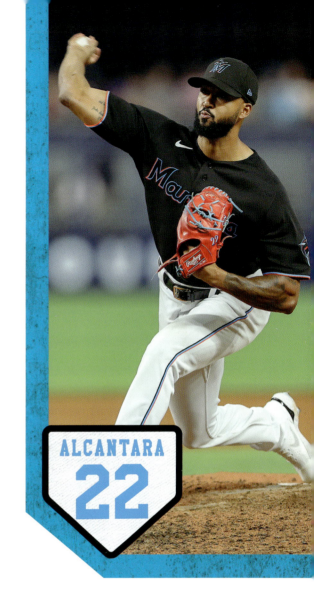

TIMELINE

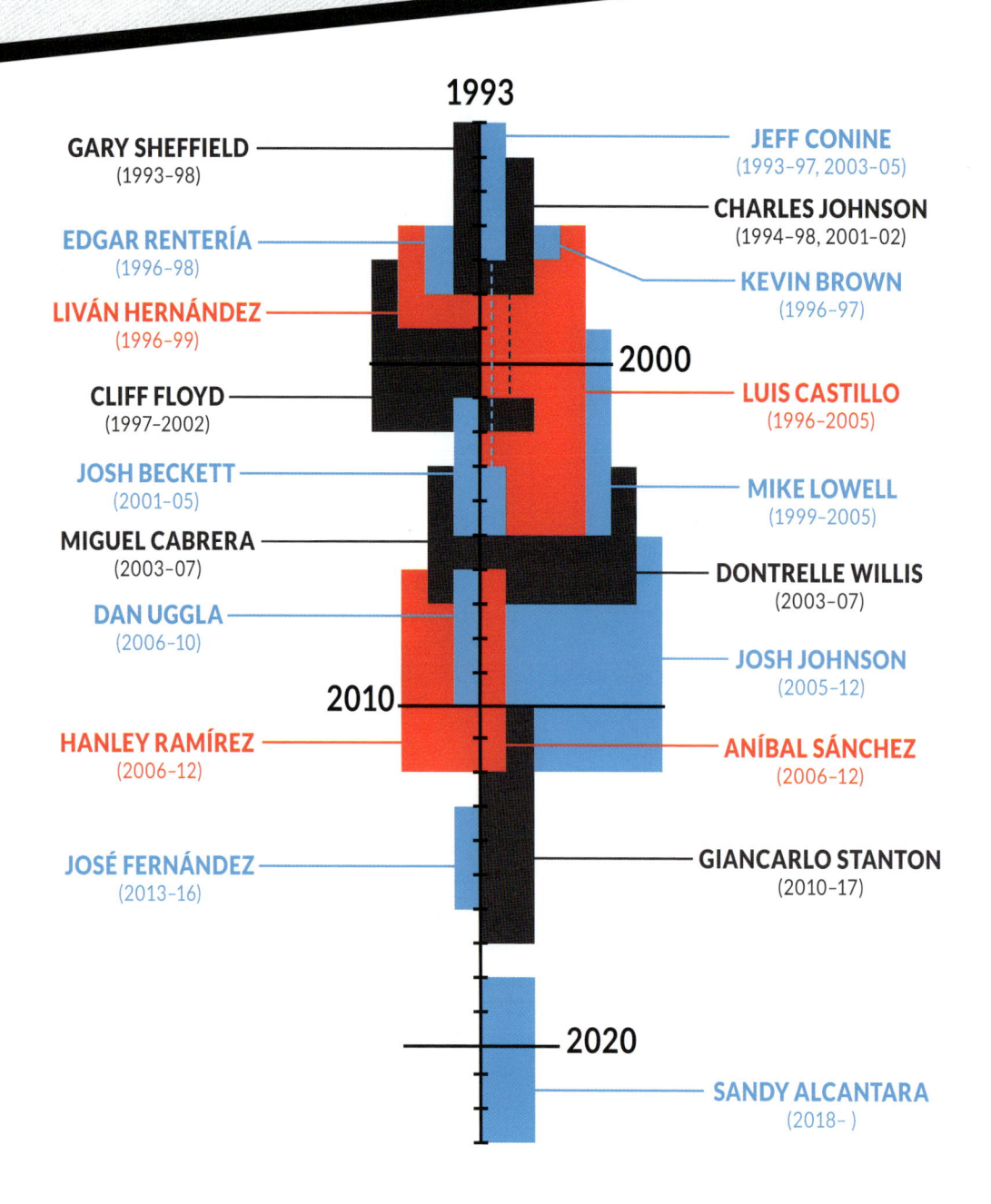

1993

GARY SHEFFIELD
(1993-98)

JEFF CONINE
(1993-97, 2003-05)

CHARLES JOHNSON
(1994-98, 2001-02)

EDGAR RENTERÍA
(1996-98)

KEVIN BROWN
(1996-97)

LIVÁN HERNÁNDEZ
(1996-99)

2000

LUIS CASTILLO
(1996-2005)

CLIFF FLOYD
(1997-2002)

JOSH BECKETT
(2001-05)

MIKE LOWELL
(1999-2005)

MIGUEL CABRERA
(2003-07)

DONTRELLE WILLIS
(2003-07)

DAN UGGLA
(2006-10)

JOSH JOHNSON
(2005-12)

2010

HANLEY RAMÍREZ
(2006-12)

ANÍBAL SÁNCHEZ
(2006-12)

JOSÉ FERNÁNDEZ
(2013-16)

GIANCARLO STANTON
(2010-17)

2020

SANDY ALCANTARA
(2018-)

TEAM FACTS

MIAMI MARLINS

Team history: Florida Marlins (1993–2011), Miami Marlins (2012–)

World Series titles: 2 (1997, 2003)*

Key managers:

Jim Leyland (1997–98)

146-178 (.451), 1 World Series title

Jack McKeon (2003-05, 2011)

281-257 (.522), 1 World Series title

MORE INFORMATION

To learn more about the Miami Marlins, go to **pressboxbooks.com/AllAccess**.

These links are routinely monitored and updated to provide the most current information available.

*through 2022

GLOSSARY

elite
The best of the best.

error
When a fielder fails to make what is considered a routine play.

expansion draft
A draft that allows a new team to fill its roster with players from other teams.

expansion team
A new team in a league, usually from a city that has not had a team in that league before.

general manager
The person in a team's front office who drafts and signs new players.

no-hitter
A game in which a pitcher, or combination of pitchers, doesn't allow any hits.

rookie
A first-year player.

walk-off
A play that ends the game.

INDEX

Alcantara, Sandy, 20–21

Beckett, Josh, 14–15
Brown, Kevin, 7

Cabrera, Miguel, 13
Castillo, Luis, 11
Conine, Jeff, 5

Fernández, José, 20
Floyd, Cliff, 12

Hernández, Liván, 8–9

Johnson, Charles, 6
Johnson, Josh, 18

Leyland, Jim, 9
Lowell, Mike, 12

McKeon, Jack, 14

Ng, Kim, 20

Ramírez, Hanley, 17
Rentería, Edgar, 9

Sánchez, Aníbal, 18
Sheffield, Gary, 5–6
Stanton, Giancarlo, 19

Uggla, Dan, 17–18

Willis, Dontrelle, 12–13